Poems for the Common Man

Words of Comfort and Inspiration

by

Betty Jo Mings

© 2002 Betty Jo Mings. All rights reserved.

No part of this book may be reproduced, stored in a retrieval system, or transmitted by any means, electronic, mechanical, photocopying, recording, or otherwise, without written permission from the author.

ISBN: 1-4033-3198-7 (electronic)
ISBN: 1-4033-3199-5 (softcover)
ISBN: 1-4033-3200-2 (hardcover)

This book is printed on acid free paper.

Scripture Quotations (unless otherwise noted) are from The Holy Bible, New International Version (NIV) © 1973, 1984 by International Bible Society, used by permission of Zondervan Publishing House.

1stBooks - rev. 9/13/02

Poems For The Common Man

I feel compelled to write my rhymes.
But I have longed, so many times,
For just a touch of eloquence,
Instead of my incompetence
At being able to express
Majestic thoughts with great finesse.
Though maybe not the way I plan,
My poems are for the Common Man,
With phrases such as "saved by grace,"
And seeing Jesus "face to face."
Just simple words to touch a life,
And help to heal heart-rending strife.

I'm sure the critics will agree
That no great poet I'll ever be.
Yet still I'll write about my Lord,
And seek His blessing as reward.
For I could have no greater gain
Than knowing I have eased some pain,
Or helped someone who's gone astray,
To come to Christ, the only way.
And so words flow—each one a prayer
That God might somehow use, somewhere,
To do His will, and fill a need.
Ah, that would bring me joy indeed!

—Betty Jo Mings

TABLE OF CONTENTS

Poems For The Common Man iii
1. Daily Living the Christian Life 1
    Choices 2
    Reflecting His Image 3
    In Simple Faith 4
    My Legacy 5
    It's Up To You 6
    Freedom In Christ 8
    Trust 9
    Psalm 15 10
    My Responsibility 11
    Sowing Seeds Of Love 12
    Faith 13
    What's That In Your Hand? 14
    Why? 15
    Your Loving Tricks 16
    My Creed For Today 17
    Planks And Specks 18
    Perfection 20
    The Battle 21
    Fruitful Branches 22
    True Freedom 23
    Psalm 73 24
2. The Church And Its Mission 25
    Our Church 26
    The Fault 27
    Prayer For Our Church 28
    Our Pastors And Their Families 29
    The Pastor's Wife 30
    Dedication 31
    A Missionary's Homecoming 32
    The Church Goes On 33
    Prayer For Our Pastor 34

3. Poems Of Comfort And Solace 35
- Never Alone 36
- My Heart Shed Tears 37
- Compassion Fatigue 38
- I Feel Your Pain 39
- Renewal 40
- You're Not Alone 41
- In His Hands 42
- Our Special Angel 43
- God Cares 44

4. Poems About The Family 45
- A Mother Who Prayed 46
- What Are You Teaching? 47
- Plenty Of Time 48
- A Sacred Duty 49
- Mother 50
- Some Things Can't Wait 51
- My Dad 52
- My Sister 53
- I Am His Child 54
- She Knelt Beside Her Bed 55

5. Poems About Friendship 57
- My Friend 58
- I Love You 59
- My Special Friend 60

6. God's Healing 61
- The Great Physician 62
- The Lord Is My Strength 63

7. Our Home In Heaven 65
- Eternity 66
- My Heavenly Surprise 67

8. Special Days 69
- A Christmas Remembrance 70

    New Year's Prayer 72
    Wise Men Still Seek Him...................................... 73

9. Maturity And Aging 75

    As I Grow Older 76
    Love's Circle 77
    The Golden Age 78
    The Wintertime Of Life 79
    After The Cataracts Are Gone 80

10. Patriotism 81

    America 82
    Freedom's Heroes... 83

11. Prayer And Praise 85

    Prayer... 86
    I Prayed... 87
    Because You Prayed 88
    Lord Keep Me Strong 89
    My Prayer For You 90
    My Symphony Of Praise 91
    Praise 92
    A Wedding Prayer... 93
    A Pilot's Prayer 94
    What Would I Do?... 95

12. Salvation And Atonement............................ 97

    Atonement's Costly Price 98
    Bread 99
    God's Perfection 100
    The Cross...101
    The Miracle Of New Birth 102
    True Riches...103
    Return To Peace..104

13. God's Love And Compassion 107

    God's Great Love 108
    Seasons Of Love..109

He Loves Me 110
God's Love 111
His Unceasing Love 112
Fashioned With Love 113
The Lord Knows 114
His Peace 115
The Lord Is Good 116
God's Peace 117
My Lord 118
I Just Have To Whisper His Name 119
My Precious Lord 120
The Sovereignty Of God 121
My Party 122

14. God's Tender Mercies 123
Forever Mercy 124
Despair And Hope 125
God's Promise 126
Joy 127
My Guardian Angel 128
My Journey Home 129
My Resolve 130
The Majesty Of God 131
The Road Of Life 132
The Way God Sees 133
Touch Any Home—It Bleeds 134
When You Can't Sleep 135
Mockingbirds 136

15. Sharing His Love 137
Did You Tell Her? 138
I Didn't Know 139
My Heart's Cry For You 140
The Answer 141
A Life In Christ 142
A Smile As Big As All Outdoors 143
Simplicity 144
A Blanket Of Love 145

Daily Living the Christian Life

Be very careful, then how you live—not as unwise, but as wise, making the most of every opportunity, because the days are evil.

Ephesians 5:15,16

Choices

I stand upon the threshold of a brand new, spotless day,
And ponder all the choices that surround me as I pray.

Because of my redemption, and my gift from God above,
Today I'm free to choose, and I've decided I'll choose *love.*

For no occasion justifies my hate or bitterness,
And love can cure a multitude of ills that cause distress.

Today I'll choose to dwell in *peace,* and quickly will forgive
Imagined hurts, and wrongful acts, so I might fully live.

I'll choose to act with *patience* as I go about my day,
And even though the wait be long, I'll use that time to pray.

I'll choose to show true *kindness* to each person that I see,
And pray that they will see the love of Christ alive in me.

Today I'm choosing *faithfulness* to promises I make,
And I will be trustworthy, and the truth I'll not forsake.

My choice is also *goodness,* and I'll strive for honesty
In every action that I take, with true humility.

Today my choice is *gentleness* in every action done,
So I'll have no regrets to feel at setting of the sun.

I'll strive today for *self control* in thought, and word, and deed,
And choose the pure and noble things on which my soul can feed.

If I have been successful with the choices I have made,
And sleep tonight with conscience free, secure and unafraid,

I'll praise my precious Lord above, Who gives abundantly
His peace that money cannot buy, and love beyond degree.

But if I fail to live today the way I know I should,
And find I've chosen what is wrong, instead of what is good,

In true repentance I will bow before my Savior's feet,
And I'll find grace and His forgiveness at the Mercy Seat

Reflecting His Image

I want my life to be a true reflection of my Lord,
And pray that I will never bring dishonor to His Name.
For those who do not know my precious Lord are judging me,
To look for any inconsistencies in what I claim.

And they examine all I do, and every word I speak,
To see if knowing Christ has brought a change that they can see.
But if I fail to live the way they think a Christian should,
I pray they won't reject salvation's gift because of me.

Please help me, Lord, to never lose my hunger for Your Word,
And keep me always focused on the One Whose Name I bear;
So when at last I meet my Savior when earth's work is done,
I'll find my life has challenged others who will meet me there.

In Simple Faith

I am not a theologian with a lot of earned degrees,
Yet I've kissed the feet of Jesus, for I've met Him on my knees.

I can't argue with the scholars on their different points of view,
But I've hovered close to Jesus as each test He's seen me through.

I don't know the many meanings of each word in Holy Writ,
But my faith's securely grounded, and I'm rich because of it.

I can't stand up in a pulpit and expound the Word with zest,
And yet I long to tell you how the Lord my life has blessed.

I'm just a simple Christian who has known the Savior's grace,
And in child-like faith I'll trust Him till some day I leave this place,

And I reach my home in Heaven on that blessed shining shore,
Where I'll be with my Redeemer and I'll praise Him evermore.

My Legacy

My life's a fleeting moment in the endless march of time,
And days on earth so soon will all be past.
I want to be remembered for the love that I have shown,
And want my legacy of love to last.

I long to share my Jesus with the people that I meet,
And pray that I'll bring honor to His Name.
I'd rather be a faithful servant of my Lord and King,
Than be endowed with beauty, wealth or fame.

I'm building for eternity, and pray my deeds won't be
Wood, hay or stubble that will quickly burn.
But if on sure foundation I use gold and precious stones,
A lasting place in Heaven they will earn.

I hope that when at last I stand before the throne of God,
There will be many others there who'll say,
"I'm here because you shared the love of Christ with me on earth,
And clearly pointed out to me The Way."

Lord, help me to reflect Your love, and like a magnet, draw
Lost, hurting souls to want to know You too.
And when my life is over, may I hear You say, "Well done.
You did your best with what I gave to you."

It's Up To You

It's not what happens to you that can make your life or break it.
The thing that really matters is the way you choose to take it.

You can have a "pity party" and say life's not worth the living,
Or find some place that needs the love and help you could be giving.

You can crawl into a shell, and reach a state of deep depression,
Or count the many blessings you still have in your possession.

You can say that life's not fair, and that you simply cannot bear it,
Or seek what's good in life, and find a way that you can share it.

No, it's not what happens that decides the winning or the losing.
It's how you take it—and you'll find it's strictly your own choosing.

Redeeming The Time

My life's too short to waste my time reliving past mistakes,
Remembering the times I've failed—my sorrows and heartaches,
I trust I won't forget my Savior died so I might live,
And since He has forgiven me, I must myself forgive.

I haven't time to spend my days in selfishness and pride,
My focus only on myself, with others shut outside,
While pushing hard to get ahead, with kindness seldom shown,
And rarely stopping to give thanks for blessings I have known.

I can't afford to hold a grudge against a one-time friend,
And not do all within my power the lack of love to end,
I want to live in harmony, in fellowship and peace,
So bitterness, and spiteful words, and hurtful deeds will cease.

And when the Lord shall call me home at setting of the sun,
I hope that I won't feel regret for things I've left undone.
But that I'll treat the ones I love with patient courtesy,
And try to show, by word and deed, how much they mean to me.

When others hurt, I want to help with diligence and grace,
And do my very best to make the world a better place.
For each day is a gift that has been given from above,
And anything is possible when hearts are full of love.

Freedom In Christ

So many souls today are bound by prisons they create,
With eyes so blinded they refuse to see.
They grope their way in darkness to a dismal, lasting Hell,
And lose their souls for all eternity.

The one locked up by prison bars, who gives his heart to Christ,
Has freedom that the world can never give.
And some day when the Lord returns to take His loved ones home,
Forever with the Lord that soul shall live.

Trust

When I recall my deep concerns,
And all my sleepless nights of yesterday,

I see God's plan, and guiding hand,
Sustaining me along my fear-plagued way.

So many trials of my life
That never were quite fully understood,

The Lord has used to strengthen me,
And work them all together for my good.

He shows His love and faithfulness
Each day I live in many countless ways;

And all He asks for is my trust,
Delighting in my love and in my praise.

I pray my faith will be so strong,
That I will worry not one single hour.

Instead, I'll trust Him for each day,
Believing He will give His peace and power.

Psalm 15

Oh Lord, I long for shelter,
  Safe upon Your Holy Hill,
So I must walk uprightly,
As I seek to do Your will.

Please keep my tongue from slander.
And let goodness flow through me.
And may my life be blameless,
While I'm nestling close to Thee.

Help me to shun all evil,
And speak truth within my heart,
So that in the time of testing,
From Your arms I'll not depart.

My Responsibility

It isn't my responsibility
To criticize and judge the things you do.
The Lord alone can look inside your heart,
And see if all your deeds are false or true.

But I'm the only one responsible
For every word and action that are mine.
And I alone am held accountable
For hurtful words that damage or malign.

And so I need to guard so carefully
The things that I allow inside my heart.
While welcoming all good and noble thoughts,
I needs must bid the evil ones depart.

And I must soak God's Word up like a sponge,
So it becomes so much a part of me,
That all my actions will be governed by
That still small voice that shows what I should be.

When constantly communing with my Lord,
I'll find the strength to live a life that's free;
And as I share His love with all I meet,
I'll thus fulfill responsibility.

Sowing Seeds Of Love

Sometimes the seeds I plant in
The garden of my life
Produce a crop of sorrow,
Unhappiness, and strife.

If I neglect to water
And feed the soil with prayers,
I scarce can find one blossom
Among the rocks and tares.

My garden needs the sunshine
God's Word supplies each day,
So I can share with others,
And point them to The Way.

Lord, send to my life's garden
Your blessings from Above;
And may I grow more like You,
While sowing seeds of love.

Faith

Sometimes God's presence seems so real...
Beyond my comprehension;
And evidence of daily help
Demands my full attention.

'Tis then I feel I understand
The way He loves and guides me,
Because I know He holds my hand,
And travels close beside me.

But other times in fear I cry,
"My God, I feel forsaken.
The storm is wild, and I'm so weak,
My faith is sorely shaken!"

But at those times, by will I choose,
No matter what my feeling,
To trust in God, believe His Word,
And go to Him for healing.

I find the less I understand
His ways, far past my knowing,
The more I learn to simply trust,
And so, my faith is growing.

What's That In Your Hand?

When Moses had fears for the journey,
God asked him, "What's that in your hand?"

"It's only a rod," said Moses;
but God had a miracle planned,

And marvelous things were accomplished
with that plain and simple rod.

It became an awesome weapon when
fully surrendered to God.

When David faced mighty Goliath, God asked,
"What's that in your hand?"

"It's only a sling," said David;
but God showed him how he could stand

And face unafraid on the hillside
that Philistine nine feet tall.

And soon the giant Goliath lay dead
from a pebble so small.

To Bunyan in Bedford Prison. God asked,
"What's that in your hand?"

"It's only a pen," John answered.
But led by the Spirit's command

He penned the book "Pilgrim's Progress";
a blessing surviving the years.

So a pen to the Lord consecrated has
helped conquer doubtings and fears.

And still God is asking the question of us,
"What's that in your hand?"

It might be a small gift He's given;
it doesn't have to be grand,

But if it is used for His glory,
His multiple blessings we'll know.

And as we surrender to Jesus,
His love and His peace He'll bestow.

Why?

I've often thought that some day I
Would meet my Lord, and ask him, Why?

Why take the dearest one I've known,
And leave me here to grieve alone?

Help me to understand just why
A child in tender youth should die

Before he's had a chance to live,
With so much talent yet to give?

And why do evil men succeed
By trampling others in their greed,

While plans of good men often fail,
With crushing grief and sore travail?

Why must God's saints endure such pain?
How can it bring eternal gain?

I searched God's Word—then wondered why
Christ died for sinners such as I?

Why did He choose to leave His throne,
And with His blood my sins atone?

Oh God, though I don't understand
The reason for the things You've planned,

I want to trust that You know best,
And in Your arms You'll give me rest,

Until I reach my home on high,
Where You'll reveal the reason why.

Your Loving Tricks

How easily you tricked me into thinking I could do
The seemingly impossible, with strength I never knew.

And when I felt like giving up, you wouldn't let me quit,
But held my hand and propped me up, and showed me I was fit

To enter life's long marathon, and run the race with pride,
While knowing if I needed you, you'd be there by my side.

You always gave encouragement when I was feeling low,
And it was your belief in me that gave me power to grow.

I look at all the things that I've accomplished through the years,
And know they couldn't have been done without your help and cheers.

Each day I count my blessings as I talk to God above,
And thank Him for the angel that is you, and for your love.

And yes, I'm thankful also for your "tricks," I must confess,
Because they were responsible for all today's success.

My Creed For Today

I won't re-live the doubt and fear that caused such pain in yesteryear.
Nor will I dwell on each mistake that brought me sorrow and heartache.

I will not wallow in despair, forgetting friends, neglecting prayer,
Till guilt sidelines me on a shelf, and all my thoughts are on myself.

For Jesus took my sin and shame, when on the cross He bore my blame.
So I must lock away the past, and seek today the things that last.

I will not wait till skies are blue to do what little I can do,
In giving help to those in need, and sharing love in word and deed.

For there is work for me to do, and each day I must start anew,
Rebuilding lives, instilling hope, in those who grieve and cannot cope.

I want to live my life each day to help lost souls to find The Way,
So when I reach my setting sun, I'll hear my blessed Lord's "Well done!"

"Do not judge, or you too will be judged. For in the same way you judge others, you will be judged, and with the measure you use, it will be measured to you. Why do you look at the speck of sawdust in your brother's eye and pay no attention to the plank in your own eye? First take the plank out of your own eye, and then you will see clearly to remove the speck from your brother's eye."

Matthew 7:1-5

Planks And Specks
(A Pharisee's Look At Life)

I look at all your faults, and I'm appalled by what I see,
And wonder why you do the things you do.
You tell me you're no worse than I, and if I'd closely check,
I'd find that I am just as bad as you.

But you are so bad tempered—almost ready to explode.
And lash out when all things don't go your way.
When I get angry, I am only angry for a cause,
And righteous indignation is okay.

You are so very proud of all the things that you possess,
And brag about your assets everywhere.
But I'm not proud like you—just have a healthy self-esteem,
Nor does my own self-image need repair.

I can't believe a word you say—you tell so many lies.
I'm sure you cheat when paying income tax.
But though I may withhold full truth, you can't call that a lie.
And why should I reveal unasked-for facts?

You gossip and you spread such tales, with untold damage done,
And sometimes lives are hurt beyond repair.
But if I tell you privately about some shameful act,
I only tell you so you'll say a prayer.

You're such a glutton when you eat, and have no self control.
You gobble almost everything in sight.
But I'm a connoisseur of food, with educated taste,
And food to me is truly a delight.

You have a judging attitude, and criticize and gripe
About the actions of all those you meet.
But I am just a fruit inspector, and I look at fruit,
To see if it is bitter, spoiled, or sweet.

You're stingy with your money, and you squeeze each dime you own,
And never want to pay your equal share.
But I am only frugal with the money I possess,
And for my later years I must prepare.

Because I am so holy, I'm concerned about your sins,
And publicly for all your faults I'll pray.
I'll pray the Lord will chastise you for all the things you've done,
And help you see the error of your way.

And then I'll offer thanks that I am filled with righteousness,
And serve my Lord in true humility.
I know He will reward me with the riches I deserve,
Because I am a perfect Pharisee!

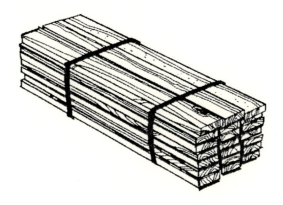

Perfection

I'm not a perfect Christian, though I try so hard to be.
The only one Who's perfect is my Lord, Who died for me.

I've tried and failed so often as the path of faith I've trod,
And I know that all my failures deeply grieve the heart of God;

Yet He puts His arms around me, and He helps me to be strong,
As He lovingly chastises me, and shows me where I'm wrong.

I'm trying to be holy, as I read the Word each day,
And I feel so close to Jesus as I bend my knees and pray,

But the times temptations lure me, and I stumble and I fall,
I must ask the Lord's forgiveness, as I hear His gentle call.

No, I'm not a perfect Christian, though I know some day I'll be
Clothed in righteousness in Heaven, as the Lord has promised me.

So I'm asking Christ to help me, just today, to do my best.
And I know if I am faithful to the task, He'll do the rest.

The Battle

I've made a lot of New Year's resolutions,
And some have not survived a single day.
Although I've had the highest of intentions,
They've somehow seemed to slowly slip away.

And endless are new leaves that I've turned over,
While planning for a spotless year ahead,
And worrying about things in the future,
With problems I anticipate and dread.

I've carried lots of weight upon my shoulders,
While searching for solutions on my own,
And sunk into the throes of deep depression,
Remembering the failures I have known.

But when at last I turned in deep contrition,
And sought the Lord's forgiveness for my sin,
I found that He would lift the heavy burden,
And give me peace and comfort once again.

He tells me not to fret about tomorrow,
But trust that He'll supply my needs each day.
The more that I surrender to His leading,
The more I am victorious in the fray.

Fruitful Branches

We live as chosen branches in the vineyard of our God,
And Jesus is the vine to which we cling.
He wants us to bear fruit that will bring glory to His Name,
And magnify our precious Lord and King.

Our Father is the gard'ner, and with love each branch He prunes,
So we can grow and show a faithful yield.
He chose us and He grafted us to draw our strength from Him,
And be a witness in His harvest field.

Each season has a purpose for the promise of the fruit;
First Springtime's growth, then Summer's ripening.
With Autumn comes the harvest, but the vine needs Winter's rest,
So it can start to grow afresh in Spring.

And so we must be faithful in the seasons that we face,
Until our lives with fruit will overflow.
For as we love each other as the Father has loved us,
In perfect peace and joy we then will grow.

True Freedom

He's locked up in a prison cell to pay the debt he owes
For many crimes against society.
And though he took no time before to read the Word of God,
His hours for reading now stretch endlessly.

At first he read the Bible just to pass the time away,
And look for any errors he could find.
But as he started searching for the things that he could mock,
He found the Scriptures touched his heart and mind.

He felt a deep conviction for the wicked life he'd lived,
And wondered if he ever could be saved.
But when he prayed the Sinner's Prayer, and asked the Savior in,
He found the peace and comfort that he craved.

He took a Bible Study Course to feed his hungry soul,
And learned to trust the Lord for all his needs.
And he became a witness to the grace that God can give
To any true repentant heart that bleeds.

He'd tell you if you asked him that he's thankful for the way
The Lord has opened up his eyes to see.
It took a prison cell to make him find eternal life,
And though he's still locked up—his heart is free!

Psalm 73

I have watched the wicked prosper,
And I've envied their success,
As they scoff, and speak with malice,
And oppress with great finesse.

While their wealth is e'er increasing,
They seem free from pain and ills.
Yet I'm chastened every morning,
Struggling just to pay my bills.

Has my heart been cleansed for nothing?
Is my innocence in vain?
This I asked the Lord in earnest,
As I wrestled with my pain.

Then my blinded eyes were opened,
And I saw their bitter end—
Utterly consumed with terror,
Desolation for a friend.

Lord, forgive my foolish envy.
Be my strength, my joy, my all.
For I know, with You beside me,
Though I stumble, I'll not fall.

The Church And Its Mission

Jesus came to them and said, "All authority in Heaven and on earth has been given to me. Therefore go and make disciples of all nations, baptizing them in the Name of the Father and of the Son and of the Holy Spirit, and teaching them to obey everything I have commanded you. And surely I will be with you always, to the very end of the age.

Matthew 28:18

Our Church

Our church is not a great cathedral filled with works of art,
With statues carved of saints and cherubim,
But just a simple edifice that's built to honor God,
And where we meet to praise and worship Him.

We don't have famous preachers clad in crested, flowing robes,
Who speak of riches and prosperity,
But only humble men of God who tell how Jesus died
To pay for all our sins, and set us free.

We have no lofty stained glass windows drawing praise of men,
Or sounds of mighty organs in our ear,
But as we lift our voices and we sing of Jesus' love,
We find the help to conquer doubt and fear.

We gather as a family to hear the Word of God,
And we are always blessed because we came.
Our fellowship and sweet communion fit us for the task
Of living to bring honor to His Name.

Our church is just for sinners who are washed in Jesus' blood,
Who try to follow Christ, His works to do.
And every one who has a need is welcome in our midst.
We pray that you will come to know Him too.

The Fault

He caught his brother in a fault,
and quickly launched a full assault.

He felt that he was duty-bound
to spread the knowledge all around.

And soon it seemed the whole world knew
about the fault, as rumors flew.

Reactions to the news were split.
Some disbelieved—but bit by bit

The church of God was torn apart
by sins that grieved the Father's heart.

If only he had gone alone,
when first his brother's fault was known,

And as they both knelt down to pray,
showed him the error of his way—

His brother might have sought God's face,
and asked forgiveness through God's grace.

The church would not have suffered shame,
nor brought dishonor to God's Name.

Instead, by faith, it would have grown,
as to the world God's love was shown.

Prayer For Our Church

Dear Lord, please bless our church today, and as we gather here,
We ask that You'll prepare our hearts to hear your message clear.

Although we are unworthy of Your Holy Name we bear,
We pray that through our lives the world will feel Your tender care.

Anoint our lips to testify of all Your love and grace,
And use our hands to aid each needy person that we face.

Help us to be responsive to the Spirit's still, small voice,
And may the way of Godliness be always our first choice.

Equip us with Your armor for the battles that we fight,
And give us strength and courage as we walk the path of light.

Increase our understanding of the Scripture that we read,
And help us not grow weary as we scatter precious seed.

We pray our church will always be a beacon to all men,
Proclaiming truth and righteousness till Jesus comes again.

Our Pastors And Their Families

Do we put them on a pedestal, and sift each word they say,
Forgetting they are sinners, saved by grace, with feet of clay?

Are we looking for perfection, and when Sunday rolls around,
Do we dine on roasted Preacher, if a single flaw we've found?

Do we watch their children carefully, inspecting every deed?
Does the slightest imperfection make us have a family feed?

Do we leave no room for error in the stringent code we set,
But play by different rules ourselves, and all our sins forget?

If we could walk a single day with them, inside their shoes,
We'd surely find that all our judging attitude we'd lose.

We'd know and understand the weighty burdens that they bear,
And we would try to help them, and to show them that we care.

We'd lift them up each day in earnest prayer before God's throne,
And ask the Lord's forgiveness when a lack of love we've shown.

The Pastor's Wife

She stands among the shadows with a smile upon her face,
And quietly encourages with love, and strength and grace.

She always offers solace, and holds tightly to his hand,
And when he feels inadequate, he knows she'll understand.

She's ready with a listening ear for what he has to say,
But things she hears in confidence she never will betray.

Their time alone is limited because he has to be
Available to all the flock who need his ministry.

Yet still she's there when like a child he clings to her embrace,
And draws upon her comfort for the trials he must face.

She is the unsung heroine who helps his load to bear,
And lifts him up consistently with tender, loving care.

The world applauds a Pastor who can help to change a life,
But half the credit for success belongs to his dear Wife.

Dedication

Dear Lord, with joy we dedicate
   This precious little child to You;
And as we seek Your help and strength,
We consecrate ourselves anew.

We pray for wisdom from above
To guide these tender, tiny feet
Along the narrow path, to find
Forgiveness at Your Mercy Seat.

Please help us teach, not just by words,
But by example that we live,
To daily search Your Scriptures for
The guidance You so freely give.

May Sundays find us worshiping
Together as a family,
As we endeavor to become
The parents You would have us be.

A Missionary's Homecoming

Returning from the mission field is quite a culture shock.
She wonders if she ever will fit in.
She looks at all the costly clothes, and cars, and fancy homes;
And finds it's worlds away from where she's been.

The sun has dried her hair, and made her skin feel rough and chapped,
And her donated clothes are out of style.
But those to whom she's ministered have known she's Heaven-sent;
She's given all, and gone the extra mile.

She never felt looks mattered there—they loved her as she was,
And many learned to love her Jesus too.
But as she comes back home she knows she doesn't quite belong,
She's feeling lost, and unattractive too.

Yet God looks deep inside her heart and sees the beauty there,
A beauty far beyond what man can see.
It comes from her devotion to the Lord Whom she adores,
And her desire to serve Him faithfully.

She needs your understanding, and she also needs your prayers,
To help with each adjustment and each test.
And as you love wholeheartedly this precious saint of God,
You'll find that you're the one who has been blessed.

The Church Goes On

He really planned to go to church.
He knew it was important, and would help him in his life,
Because of all the turmoil that he faced, and all the strife.
But somehow days just slipped away, and then the months and years,
While he kept struggling with his guilt, his problems and his fears,
And so, the church went on without him.

He said he soon would go to church.
He oft recalled the childhood times he went to Sunday School,
And how he learned John 3:16, and said the Golden Rule.
And he remembered pictures taken with his blushing bride,
While at the altar vows were said, as they stood side by side.
But now, the church went on without him.

He truly meant to go to church.
He worked so many hours each week, and when the weekend came,
He needed time just to relax, or practice his golf game.
And there were dozens of small tasks that he alone could do.
Before he even finished them, his weekend time was through.
And so, the church went on without him.

He promised he would go to church.
When friends and family begged him, he had lots of reasons why
The time was not convenient, but it would be by and by.
Soon things would settle down, and he would have more time to do
The countless tasks that he's put off, and some that were brand new.
But still, the church went on without him.

He finally went to church.
His friends all came to see him, and to say a last farewell.
And many eyes were teary as they heard his funeral knell.
They thought of all the wasted years, and blessings cast aside,
Because he thought he'd find the time for church before he died.
And still, the church goes on without him.

Prayer For Our Pastor

Lord, bless our precious Pastor as he does Your work today,
And keep him pure and righteous as he walks the narrow way.

Increase his understanding of the truths You'd have him speak,
And make him strong and fearless in the places he is weak.

Lord, give him time to study, and to read your Word, and pray,
Without the small distractions that can eat away the day.

Help him to sow with confidence, and nourish every seed,
As lovingly the Spirit speaks to hearts that have a need.

Please give him boldness to proclaim the message of Your grace.
While firmly centered in Your will, each doubt and fear erase.

And may he honor his dear wife with sweet and loving care,
To keep alive and vibrant all the tender love they share.

Dear Lord, continue using him, and bless his ministry,
With trophies of Your love that last throughout eternity.

Poems Of Comfort And Solace

Come to Me, all you who are weary and burdened, and I will give you rest. Take My yoke upon you and learn from Me, for I am gentle and humble in heart, and you will find rest for your souls. For My yoke is easy and My burden is light.

Matthew 28:18

Never Alone

Some problems are easy to handle,
And I seem to do well on my own.
But when they're too heavy to carry,
I don't have to bear them alone.

For Jesus has promised to help me,
Whenever I make my needs known.
When the terror-filled storms rage around me,
I don't have to face them alone.

Sometimes I've had strength for the battle,
And I feel that great courage I've shown.
But when fear grips my heart midst the conflict,
I don't have to struggle alone.

For I trust in my Savior to hold me,
When all my bravado has flown;
And I know He will comfort and guide me,
And He never will leave me alone

My Heart Shed Tears

Dear Lord, my heart shed tears today
Because of news about a precious friend.
Her problems seem too much to bear.
They seem to come in waves, and have no end.

You've blessed me so abundantly,
With joys far more than I could ever count.
And while I thank and praise Your Name,
The troubles for my friend just seem to mount.

My heart is sorrowing for her,
And that is why I come to You in prayer.
I'm praying You'll erase her pain,
And lift her from the depths of her despair.

To mortal mind it seems unfair,
That she should have to suffer such a loss,
While I've been basking in love's warmth,
And never had to bear so great a cross.

Lord, show me how to bless her life,
And help support the load she has to bear;
So she will see Your love in me,
And by it know how much I truly care.

Compassion Fatigue

We want to quickly change our TV stations
From scenes that have become quite commonplace,
Because we're tired of seeing starving children,
And no more homeless people can we face.

We've seen so many fires, and floods, and murders.
The nightly news is filled with tragedy.
And somehow we would like to just forget it,
If it does not affect us personally.

Dear Lord, where have we lost our deep compassion?
How have our hearts, once tender, grown so cold?
Why do we feel fatigue when viewing conflict,
And all the countless heartaches that unfold?

We ask that You'll forgive our lack of caring,
And melt our hearts, and make them like Your own.
Help us to do our best to ease the suffering,
And not to rest until Your love we've shown.

We pray we'll not grow weary in well doing,
And won't lose heart until the war is won.
But give us strength and courage for the battle,
So some day we can hear You say, "Well done."

I Feel Your Pain

I'd like to find some magic way to comfort you today.
But you have suffered such a loss—I don't know what to say.

I want somehow to let you know I hurt along with you,
And that I feel the dreadful pain that you are going through.

But words of solace don't come easy, even though I try,
And all I want to do is hold you in my arms and cry.

So even though I can't express the thoughts I feel inside,
I pray the Lord will be with you, and every need provide.

Because I know He holds you in the hollow of His hand,
I know that He will lift you up, and give you strength to stand.

Renewal

One time I had a partnership I thought would always last.
Together we would conquer worlds, till time and life were past.
But all too soon I learned that fate plays strange and cruel tricks.
And I was devastated, while my heart seemed made of bricks.

Instead of two as I had planned, I faced the world alone.
I felt unloved, and out of place; my confidence had flown.
And in a state of numbness, I existed day by day.
Because I thought that no one cared, no love I gave away.

Then one day I discovered there was much I should forgive,
If I would have my peace with God, and truly start to live.
I found the pain I had endured gave me the empathy
To stretch my hand and heart in love to those who hurt like me.

Because God never makes mistakes, the tragedy I've known
He's used to build my character, as seeds of hope He's sown.
I'm learning daily of His care, as step by step He leads.
And as I let His light shine through, He satisfies my needs.

You're Not Alone

I know that you are hurting, so I'm asking God above
To heal your broken heart, and give you peace.
I pray you'll feel the comfort of His everlasting arms,
Enfolding you with healing, sweet release.

Because I know He feels your pain, and even saves your tears,
I pray your weeping soon will turn to joy;
And that you will be free from all the irksome little things
That oftentimes embitter and destroy.

I ask for you the strength to face whatever comes to pass;
That you'll not be discouraged or depressed.
But as you wait upon the Lord, you'll feel a strengthened heart,
And He will calm your fears, and give you rest.

Remember that you're not alone, and you are dearly loved,
And you have many friends who truly care;
Who want to help you lift the heavy burden on your heart,
And constantly remember you in prayer.

In His Hands

Perhaps the Lord might come today,
to take His chosen bride away.

Then all together we would rise,
and meet our Savior in the skies.

Oh, what rejoicing there would be,
when Jesus' face we all could see!

But maybe, for my earthly span,
Christ has for me another plan.

And ere He comes to claim His own,
He might desire just me alone,

To reach my home on Heaven's shore,
and worship Him forevermore.

It could be that I'll quickly go;
and yet it might be very slow,

With many pain-filled nights and days,
while in His arms I sing His praise.

No matter what His will for me,
His love will guide me constantly.

I find each day I'm longing for
that blessed time my soul will soar.

And I will know the tender touch
of my dear Lord I love so much.

And so I pray I'll faithful be,
until the time my God I see.

Our Special Angel

God placed a special Angel in our arms for just awhile,
To scatter angel kisses, and to bless us with each smile.

Our darling little Angel brought us joy right from the start,
With little mannerisms that would fill and warm each heart.

We dreamed about the future, and the life that would unfold,
With school, and friends, and happiness, while slowly growing old.

We never could have been prepared to have our Angel leave.
And now our hearts are bruised and broken, as each day we grieve.

This tiny baby Angel, we once held so tenderly
Has left our empty arms with just a tear-filled memory.

But now we know that Heaven surely is a brighter place,
Because it has the glow of that sweet precious baby face.

And we are looking forward to our meeting on that shore,
Where there'll be no more sorrow—only joy forevermore.

God Cares

I've struggled hard to find some way that I could comfort you...
To let you know I feel the pain that you are going through.

Could gifts, or flowers ease the hurt that's tearing you apart?
Could empathizing lift the weight that lies upon your heart?

The wound is still so fresh, so raw, the agony so deep;
Relief is only brief escapes in memory or sleep.

But even death can't take away the one you've loved so much.
Because you never will forget his special, tender touch.

It just makes Heaven seem more real, to know that he awaits
The time that he can welcome you inside those golden gates.

And so with love I'll lift you up before God's Throne in prayer,
Because I know how much He cares, and that He's always there.

Poems About The Family

Love is patient, love is kind. It does not envy, it does not boast, it is not proud, it is not rude, it is not self-seeking, it is not easily angered, it keeps no record of wrongs. Love does not delight in evil but rejoices with the truth. It always protects, always trusts, always hopes, always perseveres.

1 Corinthians 13:4-7

A Mother Who Prayed

I had a Mother who prayed.
She taught me of Jesus when I was but small,
And prayed for me daily to give Him my all.
Thank God for a Mother who prayed!

I had a Mother who prayed.
She taught by example to trust in the Lord,
And live by the Bible—her spiritual sword.
Thank God for a Mother who prayed!

I had a Mother who prayed.
There wasn't much money, but when times were bad,
And someone was needy, we shared what we had.
Thank God for a Mother who prayed!

I had a Mother who prayed.
When I had a problem, and fear made me weak,
I knew on her knees God's help she would seek.
Thank God for a Mother who prayed!

I had a Mother who prayed.
And now my own children have needs, so I pray
They'll trust in the Savior, and some day might say,
"Thank God for a Mother who prayed!"

What Are You Teaching?

What are your children learning from you,
As they study your actions, and all that you do?
Are they learning that Jesus is Lord of your life—
The answer to problems and heartache and strife?
Do they learn by example to keep the Lord's Day,
And meet with His people to worship and pray?

Do they learn as they watch you, to put the Lord first,
And share Him with all those who hunger and thirst?
Do you teach them to study the Bible each day;
To keep God's commandments, and watch what they say?
The time is so short—they grow up so fast—
But all of the habits learned early will last.

Dear Parents, be careful what actions you teach,
Before it's too late, and you find you can't reach
Their hearts for the Lord, for they've gone their own way,
And made the wrong choices, and wandered astray.
A short time to teach them is given to you.
Oh, make sure your example they follow is true!

Plenty Of Time

He promised his son they would camp out all night,
Get up very early before it was light,
And go to the lake where the hungry fish bite.
But he put off the trip for the plan wasn't right.
After all—he had plenty of time.

He promised his wife they would soon get away
For a week, or a night, or just part of a day,
To rekindle the love they had let go astray.
But his work for the present left no time for play.
After all—he had plenty of time.

He promised his daughter he'd teach her to ski.
When he bought snow equipment, she shouted with glee.
But each year as she dreamed that the ski slopes she's see,
Her skis gathered dust—on deaf ears fell her plea.
After all—he had plenty of time.

He vowed to his parents he'd visit them more,
And offer his help with a much needed chore.
They lovingly looked for his face at the door,
And grieved when his absence went on as before.
After all—he had plenty of time.

He thought that one day when his life was more slow,
He'd find a good church where he wanted to go,
And learn from the Bible the things he should know,
While talent and goods on the poor he'd bestow.
After all—he had plenty of time.

His death came before some folks thought it was due,
And it shocked all his family, and friends that he knew.
So they buried him high on a hill with a view,
To watch through the seasons as life starts anew.
After all—he has plenty of time.

A Sacred Duty

That little child you're holding, Dad, who looks so much like you,
Was sent to be a blessing, but a sacred duty too.
He'll look to you for guidance as you teach him day by day,
And he will try to copy everything you do and say.

The words you use will be his words, your faults he'll duplicate,
But all the Christ-like things you do, he'll try to emulate.
Oh guard that precious little life, and watch the things you do,
So you'll be proud to have a son who'll someday be like you!

Mother

To know you
Is to know love;
Abundant,
Overflowing,
Encompassing all around you.
People may hurt you,
Neglect you,
Misunderstand you,
Yet still you love.
Your love reaches out
In tenderness,
In empathy,
In understanding.
I can't help but be
A little bit better,
A little bit wiser,
A little bit stronger,
Because I have known
Mother love
Such as yours.

Some Things Can't Wait

My house may not look perfect,
With toys on all the floors,
And crumbs upon the table,
And mess in lots of drawers;

But I took time this morning
To rock my little boy,
And read to his sweet sister.
You should have seen their joy!

My hair may not be stylish,
And I'm no fashion plate,
But love is more important.
I have my values straight!

My Dad

My dearest Dad, I love you,
And on this special day
There are so many things that
I feel, but seldom say.

You put your love in action
By all the things you do.
I've learned to live for Jesus
With trust, by watching you.

You give me Godly counsel,
With wisdom in your voice,
While still allowing freedom
To make the final choice.

The praises of another
Bring pride, and make one glad.
But these words make me proudest,
"You know, you're like your Dad."

I'm thankful for your caring,
And generosity.
I pray that God will bless you,
The way that you've blessed me.

My Sister

I know God gave you to me as a special gift of love,
To share my secret thoughts, and hopes, and dreams.
For no one else can fully understand the way I think,
Or give support for all my hopeful schemes.

We sometimes fought as children, but we made up and forgave,
And later laughed, and helped each other out.
We stood up for each other—it was us against the world,
And that our love was strong, no one could doubt.

I know you will be there for me whenever I am down,
You lift me up, and you're a loyal friend.
When others disappoint me, and I'm feeling all alone,
It's always you on whom I can depend.

I don't have to pretend to be somebody that I'm not,
For you will love me just the way I am.
You even stand behind me when I sometimes make mistakes,
And give your help when I am in a jam.

Yes, God has given blessings, much too numerous to count,
And there are many things I'm thankful for.
But there could never be a greater blessing in the world,
Than you, my Sister dear, whom I adore.

I Am His Child

I am thankful that I am a parent,
And my children are precious to me.
I have loved them with all of my being,
And cared for their needs tenderly.

They come running to me with their problems,
And believe I'll be able to find
The answers they need to help solve them,
Thus leaving their worries behind.

But I find when it's my turn for problems,
And I feel all bogged down in despair,
Then I run as a child to my Father,
And I cast upon Him all my care.

I just bask in that much needed comfort
Which only His arms can provide,
As He tenderly dries all my teardrops,
While my needs unto Him I confide.

I'm made strong when I'm helping my children,
As I draw all my strength from above;
And I know that my Heavenly Father,
Will nourish *this* child with His love.

She Knelt Beside Her Bed

I'd like to paint the picture that
I see inside my head—
A portrait of my mother as
She knelt beside her bed.

She taught me from the Bible, and
She kept me clothed and fed.
But mostly I remember times
She knelt beside her bed.

She couldn't face the world alone,
But turned to God instead,
And let Him lift her burdens as
She knelt beside her bed.

She lingered with her Savior there
And many tears were shed.
But faith became much stronger when
She knelt beside her bed.

It wasn't just the things she did,
Or even what she said.
I learned to love the Lord because
She knelt beside her bed.

Poems About Friendship

A friend loves at all times.

Proverbs 17:17

My Friend

I love you for being a true friend to me;
For all of my faults that you choose not to see.

I'm grateful I have you to lend me a hand
When I feel bogged down, and can't meet time's demand

But mostly I love you for just being there
To talk to, to listen, to show that you care.

I'll always be thankful that God chose to send
His Angel to bless me— 'tis you, my dear Friend.

I Love You

I love you for the way you always lift me up and care;
The love you so unselfishly find countless ways to share.

I love you for your thoughtfulness and sensitivity;
The beautiful example that you set for all to see.

The Lord alone knows all the special, loving things you do;
But I will always thank Him that He blessed my life with you.

My Special Friend

God blessed me in a special way
 By sending you to me one day.

You've been a dear and precious friend,
On whom I always can depend.

For all my needs you show concern,
While asking nothing in return.

And when my courage turns to fear,
You offer hope, and strength, and cheer.

I pray that all the good you do
Will be returned ten-fold to you,

And you will know God's peace and rest,
For you deserve the very best!

God's Healing

For you who revere My Name, the Sun of Righteousness will rise with healing in Its wings.

Malachi 4:2

The Great Physician

My doctor asks me how I feel,
And tells me to recite my symptoms, one and all.
The Great Physician understands,
And knows my every need before I even call.

My doctor tells me I should make
Appointments for a visit when I know he's in.
The Great Physician never sleeps,
But tells me He will stay with me through thick and thin.

My doctor tries to diagnose,
And sometimes he's concerned when he can't find a cure.
The Great Physician feels my pain,
And grieves with me, and in His love I feel secure.

My doctor uses for his tests
The best equipment he is able to provide.
The Great Physician has all power,
And all He has is mine, if I in Him abide.

My doctor sometimes makes mistakes,
Although he truly tries my sickness to arrest.
The Great Physician cannot fail,
And if He chooses not to heal, it's for my best.

My doctor always sends a bill,
So I can pay for all the service I receive.
The Great Physician freely gives
In rich abundance, all His gifts, if I believe.

My doctor tries his very best
To help me, and to satisfy all my demands.
The Great Physician holds my life,
Assuring me I could not be in better hands.

The Lord Is My Strength

I wept when I discovered that I had the dreaded "C",
And needed operations, and much chemotherapy.

I wanted God to tell me why I had to suffer so,
And all the reasons for my pain, I begged He'd let me know.

He held me in His arms, and gently brushed away my tears,
And told me He'd sustain me, and would take away my fears.

I draw upon the daily strength that's mine from God above,
For cancer is so limited, it cannot cripple love.

I find that I am able to accept my lot, and cope,
For cancer cannot take my peace, nor can it shatter hope.

It can't destroy my confidence that God is on the throne,
Or even dull the memories of blessings I have known.

It cannot silence courage, and can't quench the Spirit's flame,
And though sometimes I waver, still God's power is the same.

Each day my Lord's so precious I must marvel at His grace,
And keep on looking forward to the time I'll see His face.

Our Home In Heaven

Let not your heart be troubled; you believe in God, believe also in Me. In My Father's house are many mansions; if it were not so, I would have told you. I go to prepare a place for you. And if I go and prepare a place for you, I will come again and receive you unto Myself, that where I am, there you may be also.

John 14:1-3 (KJV)

Eternity

Please shed no tears because I'm gone
For I am with my precious Lord;
My dearest Friend, Who ransomed me,
And Who is by all saints adored.

I now can look upon His face,
Embraced by arms with nail-scarred hands.
And as I walk the streets of gold,
I hear the songs of angel bands.

There are no tears or sorrows here,
No weakness, and no grief or pain.
And if my leaving seems a loss,
Rejoice, because it is my gain!

Some day you, too, will be called home,
When earthly days will be no more,
And I'll await with outstretched arms,
To welcome you to Heaven's shore.

Life's days are short; redeem the time,
And live for Jesus faithfully,
Until we'll be again, my love,
Together for eternity.

My Heavenly Surprise

I've always loved surprises, and I find it hard to wait
To find out what is wrapped and tagged for me.
I tear into each package like an eager, happy child,
To satisfy my curiosity.

Just any little trinket brings a smile upon my face,
Because it speaks to me of loving care.
And eagerly awaiting an event is half the fun.
It doubles all the pleasure I find there.

That's why I am so anxious just to see my Heavenly home
That Jesus is preparing now for me.
He tells me that it's filled with precious stones, and streets of gold,
And water clear as crystal, flowing free.

The sun and moon won't need to shine, for Jesus is the light,
And tears and sorrows will be washed away.
And oh, the joy that's waiting when I see my Savior's face,
And enter that bright land of endless day.

I'm trying to be patient as I wait for Christ's return,
When I will rise and meet Him in the sky.
And so I do my best to live each day the way I should,
Till to His waiting arms my soul shall fly.

Special Days

There is a time for everything, and a season for every activity under Heaven.

Ecclesiastes 3:1

A Christmas Remembrance

My favorite season is here once again,
The time to remember the Savior of men,
Who left Heaven's glory to come down to earth,
And lie in a manger the night of His birth.

He came here to die, all my sins to forgive,
That some day in Heaven with Him I might live.
I look all around at the beautiful sights,
The shops and the malls with their glitter and lights;

The songs about Christmas, and sleigh bells that ring,
And children, and pageants, and choirs that sing.
And I am so busy from morning till night,
Preparing and planning to do things just right,

While shopping, and cleaning, and cooking each day,
With packages, ribbons, and cards on display,
But please help me stop, Lord, and take time for You,
And pray for Your guidance in each thing I do.

Whenever I'm baking each goodie and treat,
May I not forget those with nothing to eat.
And may I be willing to share of my wealth,
So they may be nourished, and brought back to health.

And as I send greetings to friends I love so,
Please help me to pray for Your saints I don't know,
Who suffer in prisons for bearing Your Name,
Forgotten, alone, undeserving of blame.

Each time I am cleaning to keep my home neat,
Please help me remember the ones on the street
Who shiver because they've no place to stay warm,
No shelter at all to protect from the storm.

And as I go shopping, and see the display
Of countless new garments in splendid array,
Please keep my heart tender towards people in need,
With loving compassion, devoid of greed.

When reading the Bible that tells of Your care,
Lord, give me a passion for souls in despair
Who know not the Savior Who saves them from sin.
Please help me to share, and by faith draw them in.

New Year's Prayer

Dear Lord, You've given me
   A bright New Year to start.
Another chance to be the woman
That Your love ordained I'd be.
I've asked you to forgive
My past mistakes.
And now I know I've started
With a fresh, clean page.
Transform my fumbling,
Feeble scrawls
Into Your masterpiece of love,
That reaches forth,
In spite of all my failures
And my sin,
To make my life more meaningful.
I long to be
Completely yielded to Your will.
Please help me, Lord,
To be a mirror of Your grace.
For You're my strength,
My breath,
My life.
And nothing is impossible
With you.

Wise Men Still Seek Him

Before the precious Lamb of God came down to dwell on earth,
Before the angel choruses proclaimed His royal birth,

Before the bright and shining star illumined where He lay,
Before the shepherds worshipped Jesus on His bed of hay,

Some wise men there were waiting as they watched the eastern sky,
For promised signs to signal that His birth was truly nigh.

He came to be a sacrifice for all the sins of men,
And when he rose up from the grave, He said, "I'll come again."

He promised He would take His children home to Heaven's shore,
Where there will be no sorrow—only joy forevermore.

So still the wise men of today are looking to the sky,
And longing for the time when their redemption will draw nigh.

No man can know the day or hour when Jesus will return,
But for that blessed homeward journey, hearts still wait and yearn.

He wants us to be ready, with our lamps all trimmed and bright,
As daily we walk close to Him, by faith and not by sight.

Perhaps today will be the day when we shall see His face,
And bow in humble gratitude for all His love and grace.

The night is almost over, and the dawn is breaking fast,
So we must walk in faith until we're with our Lord at last.

Maturity And Aging

Dear friends, now we are children of God, and what we will be has not yet been made known. But we know that when He appears, we shall be like Him, for we shall see Him as He is.

1 John 3:2

As I Grow Older

I pray I won't end up a grouchy old lady,
Recounting each ache and each pain
In intricate detail to all who will listen,
While hoping some pity to gain.

I pray I'll stay kind, and be helpful to others,
While striving to put their needs first;
And that I will share the sweet story of Jesus
With all who now hunger and thirst.

I pray that as years take their measure upon me,
And I grow more feeble each day,
I won't be a burden to family and loved ones,
But will bless those who happen my way.

I pray I'll not lose my keen sense of adventure,
The wonder each dawning will bring.
But that I'll find something in each day to treasure,
A joy that can make my heart sing.

I pray I'll stay focused on things pure and lovely,
Instead of the dark side of life.
And that I'll be filled with the fruit of the Spirit,
The answer to heartache and strife.

I pray that my world will be just a bit better
Because of the life that I live.
Then I'll be content when God calls me to Glory,
To know I gave all I could give.

Love's Circle

God's love is ever with us
 As seasons come and go;
From early days of Springtime,
To Winter's chilling snow.

Love's circle never-ending
Creates a spark in Spring
That glows throughout the Summer,
Its power in Fall to bring.

And when in calm of Winter,
His love, mature, o'erflows,
We then love one another,
And so the circle grows.

The Golden Age

As limbs grow feeble, and eyes grow dim,
They make me lean the more on Him.
He holds my hand, and lights my way
With love and strength for every day.

No matter where my path may roam,
Each step will bring me nearer home;
Unto the time, oh rapturous grace,
I'll see His lovely, shining face!

The Wintertime Of Life

You tell me I am old because my steps are sometimes slow;
But I have time to smell the roses, and to watch them grow.
You think my life is over 'cause my memory is dim,
But I recall the years I've loved the Lord, and walked with Him.

It's true that I don't hear so well, but still my Savior's voice
Is calling me to lean on Him, and makes my heart rejoice.
While even with my glasses it is often hard to read,
I have my large print Bible and my tapes to fill my need.

So many things I cannot do—like sew a seam, or drive,
But still I thank and praise my Lord each day that I'm alive.
He's been my close companion, and my very dearest friend,
And I'm assured He'll walk with me until my days shall end.

You know that I am old because my hair is thin and white,
But God still counts each hair, and He remains my guiding light.
No, old age isn't fun, for it brings aches, and often pain,
But when earth's days are over, there's eternity to gain.

I'm looking forward to the day I'll see my Savior's face,
So I can kneel and thank Him for His wondrous, saving grace.
Then with new voice and body I will dance, and shout, and sing
Eternal love and praises to my precious Lord and King.

After The Cataracts Are Gone

I had cataracts dimming my vision,
And a haze seemed to cover my eyes.
The whole world was dull as I viewed it;
Dark gray were the once bright blue skies.

But a miracle occurred after surgery,
And suddenly colors were bright.
My world, once so clouded in darkness,
Was filled with God's radiant light!

I thank God for repairing my vision,
And relish His marvelous grace.
But I find I am longing for Heaven,
And I'm anxious to look on His face.

Though yet I cannot see Him clearly,
Some day all the scales will be gone,
And then with new eyesight in Heaven
I'll awake to that glorious dawn.

Oh, wondrous the joys that await me,
When I shall arrive on that shore.
With clear eyes I'll see my dear Savior,
And I'll rest in His arms evermore.

Patriotism

If My people, who are called by My Name, will humble themselves and pray and seek My Face and turn from their wicked ways, then will I hear from Heaven and will forgive their sin and will heal their land.

                                        2 Chronicles 7:14

America

A lump still forms within my throat, and tears within my eye,
When I lift up my head and see Old Glory flying high.
Of songs about America, I just can't get my fill,
And patriotic marching bands will always bring a thrill.

The fact that I'm American brings gratitude and pride,
And makes me think of all I owe to those brave men who died
So I might live in freedom from oppression's stern command,
And worship God the way I choose, and seek His guiding hand.

I'm thankful for the countless blessings God has showered down,
And for the beauty manifest in every state and town.
But still I know it grieves the Lord to watch from Heaven and see
The selfish, sinful lives we lead, and our depravity.

Dear God, please bless America, and send revival fires
To heal us of our waywardness, and all our vain desires.
Show us our sins, and bring us back in worship at Your feet
To find repentance, and forgiveness at Your Mercy Seat.

Freedom's Heroes

We owe a debt of gratitude
To you, our Service Personnel,
For we are thankful for the way
You guard our shores, and do it well.

Our country calls the young and brave
To keep the torch of freedom bright,
And fight the evil that would plunge
Our world into an endless night.

But when you're on the battlefield,
Remember that you're not alone.
The Lord is fighting by your side,
With strength that you have never known.

And you are in the hearts and prayers
Of moms and dads, grandparents too,
And brothers, sisters, uncles, aunts,
Your friends and cousins who love you.

We are so very proud of you,
Who willingly pay such a price,
And we will pray each day, as you
Risk life and limb in sacrifice.

So thank you for protecting us,
So stars and stripes may proudly wave
O'er beautiful America,
The home of all the free and brave.

Prayer And Praise

I will praise You, O Lord, with all my heart; I will tell of all Your wonders. I will be glad and rejoice in You. I will sing praise to Your Name, O Most High.

Psalm 9:1-2

Prayer

I'm thankful I'm a child of God, in His safe tender care,
But most of all I'm thankful I can talk to Him in prayer.

Sometimes I come in joyful praise, and thank Him for His grace,
And other times I whisper as the tears course down my face.

I share with Him my deepest fears, my sorrows and my pain,
Until they all are washed away, much like a cleansing rain.

It often seems too marvelous to fully comprehend
The fact that Christ desires through prayer to be my dearest friend.

For in His Word He welcomes me to come before His throne,
And tells me He will answer if I make my longings known.

I've seen so many miracles that prayer alone has wrought,
But know that more would happen if I prayed the way I ought.

Dear Lord, please help me stay so close in fellowship with You,
That I'll reflect Your likeness, and draw others to You too.

And keep my heart completely tuned to hear Your every call,
So every breath will be a prayer, surrendering my all.

I Prayed

I prayed.

> I cried out in my agony, and sank in deep despair,
> And God sent bands of angels to protect and meet me there.

I prayed.

> 'Twas just the faintest whisper as I battled with my pain,
> But God gave rest and strength so I could face the world again.

I prayed.

> When I confessed my secret sins and utter worthlessness,
> Then God forgave and cleansed my heart, so He my life could bless.

I prayed.

> And God, Who knows my deepest need before I even pray,
> Already had the answer given, speeding on its way.

I prayed.

> And even though God didn't choose to grant me my request,
> Or give me what I asked for, still He gave me what was best.

I wonder what I've missed in blessings that have passed me by,
And how, through me, God could have changed my world, if only I...

> Had prayed.

Because You Prayed

You lifted up my name before God's Throne in fervent prayer
When I was feeling overwhelmed with sorrow and despair,
And God sent bands of angels to sustain and meet me there,
    Because you prayed.

You faithfully sought God's provision for my needs each day,
And prayed that He would bless me as I tried to point the way,
I felt His strength, while others fell around me in the fray,
    Because you prayed.

You sensed my need for help to solve a problem I must face,
And though you knew no details, still you asked God's love and grace,
And He provided answers, and gave me a resting place,
    Because you prayed.

I've often felt my faith renewed, with doubts and fears relieved,
And been amazed to feel God's power, and all that's been achieved,
And so I kneel and thank the Lord for blessings I've received,
    Because you prayed.

Lord Keep Me Strong

I pray, dear Lord, You'll keep me strong,
When times are tough, and things go wrong.
Help me to tightly grasp Your hand
When problems I don't understand
Send waves of doubt upon my soul,
And make me feel I've lost control.

Give me the faith to clearly see,
Through whirlwinds of adversity,
The One Who leads me day by day,
And helps me walk the narrow way.
Though others may abandon You,
I pray for courage to stay true.

Remove the terror ling'ring near,
And send me faith that conquers fear.
May every trial I must go through
Just draw me closer, Lord, to You.
And help my feet to never roam,
But follow as You lead me home.

My Prayer For You

Today I lifted up your name
  Before the Lord in prayer.
I asked Him to supply your needs,
And keep you in His care.

I pled with Him to make you well,
And take away your pain;
To chase away your sorrows, as
The sunshine chases rain.

Because I know He holds you in
The hollow of His hand,
I prayed that you would know His peace,
And have the strength to stand.

If you should be discouraged, and
Feel moored in deep despair,
Please know I dearly love you, and
Remember you in prayer.

My Symphony Of Praise

Lord, make my life a symphony
Of praise—an offering.
Remove each strident, squeaky chord,
And sweeten every string.

Please keep the instruments I play
Attuned in harmony,
So no discordant notes can spoil
The finished melody.

And keep me centered on the One
Who leads with matchless grace;
And after life's crescendos fade,
Provides a resting place.

Praise

My precious Lord, I love You, and I offer praise to You
For choosing me to be Your child, and for the things You do.

I talk to You throughout the day, and sometimes through the night.
With loving arms You cradle me, and take away my fright.

I never have to walk alone, for You are by my side,
Encouraging and comforting, my stumbling steps to guide.

Although I cannot fully comprehend salvation's plan,
Or why the earth's Creator chose to die for sinful man,

I thank You for the love that bore the cross, my debt to pay,
And for the sacred blood that flowed to take my sins away.

My heart finds solace just to know that You've prepared a place
Where some day I will live with You, a trophy of Your grace.

You've been so wonderful to me, so faithful through the years,
Supplying all my deepest needs, and drying all my tears,

That praises seem inadequate; mere words cannot express
My thankfulness and awe at Your majestic holiness.

I can but sing a song of love, a hymn of heartfelt praise,
As humbly I bow down to You in worship all my days.

A Wedding Prayer

Dear Lord, please bless our union as
We start our married life.
We pray we'll live unselfishly
As husband and as wife.

Please keep our love alive and strong;
Its joy renewed each day.
And make us tender, sweet and kind
In all we do and say.

We pray we'll both be faithful to
Each other, and to You.
May our commitment grow with time,
Until our life is through.

A Pilot's Prayer

Dear Lord, I ask for guidance as
I chart my course through life;
And help me find Your flight plan, that
Will conquer pain and strife.

I know there is no lapse rate in
The warmth of Your great love.
Keep open, free and clear my lines
Of guidance from Above.

And as I face the slips and skids
Of daily life, I pray
My turn coordinator will
Stay centered on Your way.

But most of all, remind me You're
The Pilot In Command,
And I'm a flight crew member, held
In Your protective hand.

What Would I Do?

In prison Paul and Silas sat with feet in stocks secured,
Their backs were bruised and bleeding from the flogging they'd endured.
And yet they sang and praised the Lord throughout the midnight hour,
And all the other inmates heard and felt the Spirit's power.
The jailer and his household came to trust the Lord that night,
And found that knowing Christ was both a joy and a delight.

I wonder how I would respond if tragedy befell?
Would I still trust and praise the Lord, and of His goodness tell?
Or would I scream and rant and say to God, "It isn't fair!"
And ask Him why He let me down, as if He didn't care?
And would I turn my back on Him, complaining all the while,
With angry, bitter words, and never once a cheerful smile?
And maybe stop attending church, or reading from His Word,
Or even care to share His love with those who've never heard?

I pray I would believe that God was working for my best,
And that I would be strong and faithful as I faced each test.
For even though my heart was breaking, I could rest secure
In knowing God would give me strength, and help me to endure.

Salvation And Atonement

If you confess with your mouth, "Jesus is Lord," and believe in your heart that God raised Him from the dead, you will be saved. For it is with your heart that you believe and are justified, and it is with your mouth that you confess and are saved.

Romans 10:9-10

Atonement's Costly Price

The twelve who followed Jesus didn't really know
When Jesus knelt and washed their feet before He died,
That soon they would be washed completely in the blood
Which flowed on dark Golgotha from His wounded side.

The bitter cup of sorrow by His choice He drank,
To pay the awful penalty of sin's demand.
And only when He rose triumphant from the grave,
And conquered death forever did they understand.

And still today men scoff, and fail to comprehend
Atonement's costly price—salvation's simple plan.
They follow vain philosophies with blinded eyes,
And scorn the God who came to earth to ransom man.

But those who bear His Name can share communion's cup;
A symbol of the precious blood He freely gave
As sacrifice, so all who choose to come and drink
Will be made whole, and never need to fear the grave.

Bread

Mere bread cannot my cravings satisfy.
Though glutted and o'er filled my body be,
My hungry soul cries out for Living Bread
To fill my heart, and set my spirit free.

As Jesus blessed and multiplied the loaves.
And fed the hungry hordes in Galilee,
I seek fulfillment from the Bread of Life
To feed this hunger that's a part of me.

I see that precious, holy body pierced
And broken on the cross by sinful men.
And as I eat Communion's broken bread,
I celebrate Christ's victory over sin.

Oh Father God, I long to daily eat,
And share Your Bread with all who do not know.
Please bless and multiply this Holy fare,
Until its imprint on my life I show.

God's Perfection

From nothing God created all the Heavens and the earth,
And breathed the breath of life in man, and loved him from his birth.
        Perfect Divinity.

And then God sent His Son to earth, to live among the strife.
He healed the sick, and raised the dead, and lived a sinless life.
        Perfect Humanity.

Although He was the Son of God, a servant He became.
He washed the feet of His disciples, seeking no acclaim.
        Perfect Humility.

He made salvation's plan so clear a child could understand.
He bade the children come to Him, and take Him by the hand.
        Perfect Simplicity.

He taught the Bible's secrets to His loved and chosen few.
And every time one reads it, all the words are fresh and new.
        Perfect Complexity.

He died upon a cross of shame to save us from our sin,
And opened up the gates of Heaven to invite us in.
        Perfect Victory.

Someday He'll call His loved ones home, to live forevermore,
And be with Him forever on that bright and shining shore.
        Perfect Eternity.

The Cross

I Cringed with horror at the wicked men
Who crucified the Lord at Calvary.
I wondered how their hands could drive the spikes
That held His limbs secure upon the tree.

Then Jesus looked at me with love, and said,
"My child, it was for *you* I had to die.
It was *your sins* that put me on the cross,
And for *your life* I paid that price so high."

I wept, and prayed, and asked Him to forgive
My sinful heart, and write my name above.
He heard my prayer, and I was born again.
My soul He ransomed with His tender love.

Oh Lord, I pray I never will forget
The awful punishment for me You bore.
Please keep my heart attuned to hear Your voice,
Until my soul finds rest on Heaven's shore.

The Miracle Of New Birth

I watched a hairy caterpillar crawling on the ground.
It slowly inched its way along, not making any sound.
To me it looked quite ugly, and I thought, "I'd hate to be
A worm-like creature such as that, who crawls painstakingly."
But as I watched, it slowly found a limb, and held on tight,
And spun a silk cocoon that kept it safely out of sight.
And then one day it struggled to break free so it could fly,
And I beheld a butterfly that rose up to the sky.
Its beauty was spectacular, and now its wings could soar,
For days of crawling in the dirt were gone forevermore.

I pondered on the wonder of that glorious new birth,
And thought of how the Lord looks down upon our sin-sick earth.
We must resemble lowly worms who wallow in our sin,
But that is why Christ came to earth, to save the souls of men.
He wraps us in His loving arms, and writes our names above,
And we become new creatures, born again by His great love.
And someday we will leave this earth, and with our wings we'll fly
 With beautiful new bodies to our mansions in the sky.
For God has wrought a miracle in those He chose to be
His holy bride, to reign with Him through all eternity.

True Riches

You look at me as poor, because I have no money left for frills.
But I am rich! My Father owns the cattle on a thousand hills!

You think I'm unimportant, for I have no earthly claim to fame.
But God, the maker of the universe, knows me, and calls my name!

He gives me strength and comfort, and He feeds my soul with living bread.
He gently binds my wounds, and even counts the hairs upon my head.

Although I'm just a sinner, and could never pay Salvation's price,
God's Precious Lamb died in my place, and thus became my sacrifice.

Yes, I am rich! And I am loved, far more than earthly tongue can tell!
For I belong to Christ, my blessed Lord Who conquered death and Hell.

And so I anxiously await the day when I shall see His face,
And falling down in worship, I will thank Him for His love and grace.

And there will be no tears or sorrow in that home on Heaven's shore,
Where I will live with Jesus, and will love and praise Him evermore.

Return To Peace

I quietly slipped through the dew-laden dawn,
A carpet of leaves 'neath my feet.
The years fell away, and a youth I became;
The world an adventure to meet.

How oft in my dreams I'd returned to this place,
To conscience as yet undefiled
By appetites sated, and lusts satisfied;
To innocence known as a child.

I longed to reclaim the exuberant joy
I'd felt at the first sign of Spring;
To hold and examine a delicate bud,
And listen for robins to sing.

But conscience relentlessly made me recall
The shambles I'd made of my life.
The hearts I had broken, the souls I had wronged,
My anguish, and heartache, and strife.

I thought of the Jesus my parents had loved;
The God I'd rejected with scorn.
I dropped to my knees, and my beautiful glen
Became a cathedral that morn.

I opened my heart, and I poured out my soul,
And begged God's forgiveness from sin.
And just as He promised, the Giver of life
Gave me a new heart, and came in.

My heart was unburdened; my cares rolled away,
In those precious moments of prayer.
And nothing before it, or since that I've known
Could equal the peace I felt there.

Now, more than just mem'ries of childhood delights
Are drawing me back to that place.
For there, while the angels of Heaven rejoiced,
I claimed God's great love, and His grace.

God's Love And Compassion

The Lord is gracious and compassionate, slow to anger and rich in love. The Lord is good to all; He has compassion on all He has made.

Psalm 145:8

God's Great Love

There's light at the end of each tunnel,
And sunshine that comes after rain.
The darkest of nights ends with morning,
And God sends relief from all pain.

Our sorrows won't grieve us forever,
And heartaches will vanish with time.
Each burden we bear will be lifted,
And mountains made easy to climb.

The Lord will send strength to sustain us,
As much as we need for each day.
His arms will enfold and uphold us,
And answers will come when we pray.

He wants us to faithfully trust Him,
And send forth our praises above.
The closer we draw to the Savior,
The more we'll experience His love.

Seasons Of Love

As dawn chases darkness,
And sun cancels rain,
God's love eases sorrow,
And banishes pain.

As fresh as the Springtime,
When green shoots appear,
His love cools the heat-waves
Of Summer, and fear.

We change like the Autumn,
Grow cold as the snow;
But God's love is constant—
A sure, steady flow.

Lord, help me to mirror
The love that You give,
So through every season,
In me it will live.

He Loves Me

When I have no strength to stand,
And I cannot understand
Why the Lord allows such suffering in my life.
I'm reminded in God's Word,
That my prayers will all be heard,
And He'll see me through each heartache, pain and strife.

When I've failed to meet some test,
And my heart can find no rest,
And I feel o'erwhelmed, defeated, and alone;
Then the Spirit's still, small voice
Shows me how I can rejoice,
For the cleansing with repentance I have known.

When a friend becomes a foe,
And my problems seem to grow,
And my pure intentions are misunderstood,
Jesus calms my doubts and fears,
And He dries away my tears,
While He turns things planned against me into good.

If I read God's Word each day,
And I trust Him and obey,
And I keep in constant touch with Him in prayer,
I can win against each foe,
And His peace my life will show,
For He loves me, and He'll keep me in His care.

God's Love

God loved me in the Springtime,
When life was fresh and new.
Though I was weak and childish,
His caring saw me through.

God loved me in the Summer,
When I would plunge headlong
Through all my foolish choices,
Yet still His love was strong.

God loved me in the Autumn.
Each time I turned around
And asked for His forgiveness,
His steady arms I found.

God loves me in the Winter.
Each day I feel love's glow.
I'm constantly astounded
That He should love me so!

His Unceasing Love

No matter how often I stumble,
The Lord holds me up lest I fall
He always is ready to help me,
And answer whenever I call.
    Unfailing love!

Sometimes I feel close to my Savior,
Delighting in praising His name.
But when I grow cold in my ardor,
His caring for me stays the same.
    Unchanging love!

No angel, or demon, or power
On earth or in Heaven above,
Or things in the present or future
Can separate me from His love.
    Unconquerable love!

Fashioned With Love

Great God, from Your own place, You look at me on earth.
You fashioned with Your love my heart before my birth.

You know my secret thoughts, and understand my pain.
Your love directs my steps in sunshine and in rain.

You hear and answer prayer before I even ask.
And give me help each day, with strength for every task.

Oh blessed, holy God, in humbleness I bow,
And thank You for the grace that overwhelms me now.

Forgive my wayward sins, and keep my heart today
Surrendered to Your will, and turned towards You, I pray.

The Lord Knows

The Lord knows all the grief and pain you suffer,
  For He became a man and suffered too.
Because He feels your sorrow and your heartache,
He wants to give His peace and rest to you.

Just lean on Him, and let Him bear your burdens,
And trust Him, for He knows what's best for you.
Believe His Word, and claim each precious promise,
For everything He promised He will do.

His Peace

The Lord gives me strength when I'm sad and discouraged.
His love sees me through every problem I face.
When my long night is spent with a river of weeping,
He rolls back the clouds with His sunshine of grace.

When pressured with burdens I'm too weak to carry,
Besieged on all sides, and expected to fail,
His peace fills my soul like a stream in the desert,
So to a safe harbor my frail craft can sail.

Though sometimes I slip, and I make the wrong choices,
And guilt like a millstone starts holding me down,
I fall on my knees, and I beg His forgiveness.
He offers me life, and a home, and a crown.

The Lord Is Good

My trials came and crushed me down
So low, I didn't have the strength to stand.
I felt life's meaning all was gone;
That shattered were my dreams, and all I'd planned.
Through endless days and nights I tried
To understand why God allowed such pain.
I felt defeated and alone,
And that I never would be whole again.
But in a still, small voice God spoke,
As I fell on my knees and sobbed a prayer.
I felt His loving arms enfold,
And lift me from the depths of my despair.
PRAISE GOD! THE LORD IS GOOD!

I never knew in those dark days
The things that God was planning for my life,
Or just how close to Him I'd grow,
While groping through my heartache, tears and strife.
Or that God soon would send my way
Some others who were hurting just like I;
And I could share their agony,
And help them understand the reason why.
Oh Lord, I thank you for the way
You've worked all things together for my best.
If I had known no suffering,
Then others' lives through me could not be blessed.
PRAISE GOD! THE LORD IS GOOD!

God's Peace

Some times God calms the storm,
And turns it clear and mild.
Some times He lets it rage,
And calms, instead, His child.

Though tempests round me pound
Through terror-ridden night,
The Lord will give His peace,
And love away my fright.

My Lord

How I love my precious Lord,
Heaven's gift, by saints adored;
Gift I never could afford.
    He gives!

I can't wander from His care,
For His love is always there,
Saving me from deep despair.
    He loves!

I don't have to sink in guilt
In a prison I have built.
That is why His blood was spilt.
    He forgives!

He removes my sins from me,
Deeper than the deepest sea,
Where for all eternity,
    He forgets!

And some day I'll live with Him,
With the saints and cherubim.
There His light will never dim.
    He reigns!

I Just Have To Whisper His Name

I opened my heart up to Jesus.
He saved me, and life's not the same.
And now when I need help and comfort,
I just have to whisper His Name.

He's dearer than all of life's treasures.
He's greater than all earthly fame.
Each promise is mine for the asking.
I just have to whisper His Name.

Friend, turn your life over to Jesus.
His precious salvation now claim.
And some day He'll take you to Heaven.
You just have to whisper His Name.

My Precious Lord

When daily toils and trials increase,
My Lord gives His abiding peace.

When once-dear friends forsake and flee,
I feel His arms enfolding me.

When I feel lost and all alone,
'Tis then His tender love is shown.

When no one's near to hear my cry,
I know my precious Lord is nigh.

Though I sink low in deep despair,
He shows again His constant care.

When no more pain can I endure,
He gives me hope, steadfast and sure.

And as I lift my heart and pray,
I feel His strength anew each day.

He leads and guides each step I take,
And tells me He will not forsake

And as I read His Word He feeds
My hungry soul, and fills my needs.

He gives me grace, and so much more!
Some day my ransomed soul shall soar,

And In God's loving arms I'll be
Secure for all eternity!

The Sovereignty Of God

I cannot comprehend this grief that I am forced to bear.
I've asked the Lord to tell me why He doesn't seem to care.
My tears flow like a river, while my heart constricts with pain,
And all the joy that once I knew, it seems I can't regain.

The only solace I can find is going to God's Word,
Where I'm assured I'll find the help to calm and undergird.
But still I find God's sovereignty I'll never understand,
And I will never know the reasons for the things He's planned.

I only know He loves me, and is working for my best.
And He has promised if I'm faithful, He will give me rest.
While drawing on His comfort, that my empty heart can fill,
I find that I'm a partner in the working of His will.

The Master Potter knows I'm weak, and have no strength to stand,
And yet He is remolding me, with sure and steady hand.
He's making something beautiful from my life's damaged clay,
And He will wrap me in His love, with strength to face each day.

My Party

I planned an exclusive party.
I worked on my plans slavishly.
The theme of my party was "pity"
And the only guest was "poor me."

I dwelt upon each hurt and sorrow,
And probed all the problems I faced,
While each of the slights I had suffered
Around me I carefully placed.

I spent endless hours in my misery,
Recalling the depth of each pain,
As each reappeared it grew larger,
Thus causing more pity to gain.

The longer I stayed at my party,
The more I felt sorry for me.
And the lower I sank in depression,
The less of real hope I could see.

I reluctantly opened my Bible,
And read of God's love and His grace.
The Lord touched my heart at that moment,
As tears coursed their way down my face.

I started to count all my blessings,
And realized as never before,
That when I think they're all numbered,
The Lord keeps on giving me more.

I prayed to the Lord for forgiveness
For failing His mercy to see.
Now I ask you to join my new party
And celebrate God's goodness with me!

God's Tender Mercies

The Lord is full of compassion and mercy.

James 5:11b

Forever Mercy

The earthly things I think will last just crumble and decay.
They break and cease to function as they slowly rot away.

Relationships that seem so strong and destined to endure,
Soon fade away to nothingness, without a hope of cure.

But only God's great mercy will withstand the test of time.
It guides me and upholds me as I feel His love sublime.

I sin and need forgiveness, and I go to Him in prayer.
He gives me strength and comfort, and His mercy's always there.

When life seems overwhelming, and I don't know where to turn,
His mercy calms my fears, and gives the peace for which I yearn.

When each day is a struggle, filled with sickness and despair,
I'm strengthened by His mercy, as I cast on Him my care.

I praise Him for His mercy that comes fresh and new each day,
Surrounding and sustaining me as close by Him I stay.

Despair And Hope

Dear Lord, I'm really hurting, and my heart is filled with fear.
Your mercy I am questioning, and doubts are lingering near.

I've reached the end of every dream and every shattered hope,
And find that with this avalanche of problems I can't cope.

My pillow drips with sorrow as my tears flow all night through,
While I have lost the confidence and joy that once I knew.

I feel alone and desperate, so Lord, please help me find
A message from Your Word to calm my fears and ease my mind.

I read that You'll supply my need, and close by me You'll stay,
And You will give me all the strength I need for each new day.

You tell me all my fears and sorrows I can bring to You,
And as I talk to You in prayer, Your love will shine anew.

There are so many promises Your Word to me has shown,
And as I read I gain the power to claim them as my own.

Please, Lord, forgive my lack of faith, and help me never stray
Beyond the shadow of Your grace, or from Your hand away.

I thank You for the depths of Your great love, and for Your care,
And for my home in Heaven and the place You now prepare.

Please help me to be ready when You come to claim Your bride,
As we arise to reign with You, forever by Your side.

God's Promise

The Lord has promised comfort for
  My times of deep despair.
He promised if I truly seek Him,
He will meet me there.

My tears are precious to Him, and
He feels my grief and pain.
He gently binds my wounds, and turns
My losses into gain.

He tells me He will work all things
Together for my best.
If I just learn to lean on Him,
Then He will do the rest.

He always will be there for me,
No matter where I roam,
Until some day He takes my hand,
And leads me safely home.

Joy

The world is all aglow
  With temporary pleasures,
Which it would have you think
Are really priceless treasures.

But all too soon the gloss
Has disappeared or faded;
For hopes once high have sunk,
And left you feeling jaded.

The world will tell you how
To gain the joy you're after
Through mind control escapes,
Or ego boosts and laughter.

But if you seek true joy
You'll find in Sacred Pages,
It springs from Christ alone,
And lasts through endless ages.

My Guardian Angel

I have an angel guarding me, who never makes a sound,
But since I came into the world, he's always been around.

Oft times when there was danger, his protectiveness I've known,
His wings enfolding, lest I dash my foot against a stone.

Because my Heavenly Father cares about each thing I do,
He sent my guardian angel to protect my whole life through.

I often breathe a prayer of thanks when danger has passed by,
Because of help that I've received in bountiful supply.

But usually I never know the things he's saved me from,
Or all the times he's given help so I could overcome.

And when I read the Bible I'm assured that he is there,
A beautiful example of my Father's love and care.

And some day when my work is done, and life on earth is o'er,
We both will kneel at Jesus' feet, and praise Him evermore.

My Journey Home

I cried to God, "This pain is more than I can bear!"
He said, "I'll ease your pain; just cast on Me your care."

I said, "I've sinned so much that I don't care to live."
He said, "Confess your sins. I'll cleanse you and forgive."

I said, "The road is dark... impossible to see."
He gently said, "All things are possible with Me."

I said, "But I'm afraid that I will lose my way."
He said, "I'll lead you home if close to Me you'll stay."

I said, "But I'm so tired... I'm weary and depressed."
He said, "Come unto Me, and I will give you rest."

At last I said, "Dear Lord, I'm Yours... please take control.
He said, "Just lean on Me, I'll heal and make you whole."

My Resolve

I refuse to let the problems that I'm facing get me down.
I'll not walk around discouraged with a sad, unhappy frown.

I won't let myself be angry, or immersed in bitterness,
But I'll seek to show forgiveness to the ones who cause distress.

For I know my Savior loves me—that He holds me in His hand,
And He knows the reason for the things I cannot understand.

When I read His precious promises, I know His Word is true.
And everything that He has promised He will surely do.

He'll help me to survive this pain, and give me faith to trust,
So I can face my life with hope. I can, I will, I must!

The Majesty Of God

I cannot comprehend the awesome majesty of God,
Who fashioned the vast universe, and flung the stars in space;
A God who loved and chose me long before the earth was framed,
And proved His love by saving me, and dying in my place.

His greatness is inscrutable, beyond this finite mind,
And nothing in my knowledge can begin to understand
How He with His omniscience guides each stumbling step I take,
And with divine omnipotence holds fast my trembling hand.

How could the great Creator have such patience with this child;
To hold me in His arms, and save each tear that I have shed?
How could He know and care about each little thing I do,
And know my thoughts, and even count each hair upon my head?

To fathom such unbridled love is far beyond my ken,
And to all mortal minds it will remain a mystery.
I can but bow my head in humble gratitude and thanks,
That I will live some day with Him through all eternity.

The Road Of Life

My tear-dimmed eyes were cloudy as I stumbled down the road.
I felt depressed and lonely as I struggled with my load.
I couldn't see the sunlight for my head was hanging low,
And endless seemed the path because my troubled steps were slow.

But when I looked up to the hills, my burdens slipped away,
And I beheld God's glory as my heart began to pray.
I felt God's arms around me while He filled my soul with peace,
And as I worshipped Him my earthly worries seemed to cease.

He told me He'll sustain me if I cast on Him my care,
And help for all my problems is no further than a prayer.
I still must walk the path of life, but now I have no fear,
For Jesus guides each step I take, and help is always near.

The Way God Sees

I look and see a helpless child, who's weak and insecure.
God sees a mighty saint of God, with faith that's strong and sure.

I see a mountain in my path, too high, too wide to span.
God sees the tunnel going through according to His plan.

I see the failures in my life, that all the world can see.
God sees my failures turned to gain, my loss to victory.

I see the wild and stormy seas, with waves that crash and roar,
God sees the lighthouse guiding me in safety to God's shore.

I see small puzzle pieces of life's picture that I face,
God sees the final masterpiece, with each small piece in place.

Although my earth-dimmed eyes can't see the plan God has for me,
I know He'll help me to be strong, and win the victory!

Touch Any Home—It Bleeds

Some people seem to be so blessed.
Of earthly things, they own the best.
They seem a shade above the rest.
   But when you touch their home—it bleeds.

And some folks have a lot of pride.
But you don't know the pain they hide,
Or all the hurt they feel inside.
   And if you touch their home—it bleeds.

Some paste a smile upon their face,
And you admire their charm and grace.
But they have guilt they can't erase.
   And when you touch their home—it bleeds.

No matter what a man is worth;
Despite great fame, or noble birth,
For everyone who lives on earth,
   When you but touch his home—it bleeds.

That's why we need our Savior's care,
To heal our sorrows and despair;
A loving Friend Who's always there,
   For times our home is touched—and bleeds.

When You Can't Sleep

When you can't get to sleep, and you tumble and toss,
While your mind dwells at length on a pain, or a loss,

Try making a list of the blessings you've known,
Those numberless times that God's love has been shown—

The things in your life you have not understood,
That taught you to trust, and worked out for your good.

Your sleep will be restful, your worries will cease,
And all through the night you will feel God's sweet peace.

Then when you wake up, and you start a new day,
Take note of each blessing that brightens your way.

And as you say "thank you" for each, one by one,
You'll find that your list will expand, ton by ton.

Mockingbirds

I'm thankful for the mockingbirds, and for their notes of cheer,
For even in the darkest night their songs tell me they're near.

Somehow my heart is comforted with each clear melody,
For it reminds me how my Father loves and cares for me.

Each lily of the field is clothed in beautiful array,
And I see God's protectiveness in Nature's vast display,

But nothing means so much to me, or touches my heart more,
Than hearing from the mockingbirds their sweet and varied score.

If I should feel discouraged over losses I have known,
The birds outside my window let me know I'm not alone.

So when I count my blessings God bestows abundantly,
The mockingbirds rate special thanks for joy they give to me.

Sharing His Love

I consider my life worth nothing to me, if only I may finish the race and complete the task the Lord Jesus has given me – the task of testifying to the Gospel of God's grace.

Acts 20:24

Did You Tell Her?

She dries her tears, and tries to place
A happy smile upon her face.
With practiced skill in make-up, she
Removes her signs of misery.
Her suffering she dare not show,
And those at work must never know.

Most envy her enchanted life,
And never dream it holds such strife.
She feels so lost, and all alone,
Remembering the hurt she's known.
She thinks nobody knows, or cares,
And so her pain she never shares.

But Jesus knows each tear she's cried,
And for those tears He bled and died.
He longs to every doubt destroy,
And turn her weeping into joy.
He wants to live inside her heart,
And bid her anxious fears depart.

But if we don't our Savior share,
How can she ever know His care?
How sad her words when life is through,
"You told me not. I never knew!"

I Didn't Know

I watched you as you went about your business.
You seemed to have your future well in hand.
I must admit I felt a trace of envy.
I thought you had the world at your command.

I didn't know the pain that you were feeling,
Or that your world was caving in on you.
And so I didn't offer you compassion,
As daily all your fears and troubles grew.

Forgive me for my seeming lack of caring.
I would have tried to help, had I but known.
If I had listened to your heart's deep pleading,
More love and tenderness I would have shown.

But now it is too late to try to reach you,
For you are far beyond all earthly care.
I'm sorry that I failed you so completely,
And of your mental state was unaware.

With tears I've prayed, and asked the Lord to help me,
To know when others hurt—to be aware,
So I can share the precious love of Jesus,
And help them find and trust His tender care.

My Heart's Cry For You

I found a priceless treasure when I met the God of love,
And asked Him to forgive my sins, and write my name above.
Oh, how I long for you, my Friend, to know my Jesus too;
To have Him take away your sins, and make your heart brand new

I long for you to know the joy of having answered prayer,
To know He cares for you so much he numbers every hair.
I pray that you will feel the peace that Christ alone can give,
To be assured He'll care for you as long as you shall live.

I pray you'll know for certain where you'll spend eternity,
For Jesus has prepared a home above for you and me.
But oh, the sorrow that awaits for those who don't believe—
Eternal punishment in Hell if Christ you don't receive.

And that is why, my precious Friend, I pray for you each day,
And why, with tears, I've tried so hard to point you to The Way.
You have to make a choice regarding your eternal fate.
Oh, ask the Lord to save your soul before it is too late!

The Answer

The whole wide world is hurting.
  Sad souls are crying out,
And asking for an answer
To heartaches, fears and doubt.

They meet complacent Christians
Why hurry through each day,
And never think to tell them
About the Living Way.

Dear Lord, please make me different,
With sensitivity,
To be a caring channel
To point my friends to Thee.

I want to share the Gospel,
And help them trust in You,
So when I meet my Savior,
I'll know they'll be there too.

A Life In Christ

I met an old man, sick and worn,
  Whose life was almost gone.
I led him to the Lord of life
Before he journeyed on.
With fainting breath, and feeble lips,
His heart believed at last;
But oh, too soon death came to reap,
And then his days were past.

I met a woman half way down
The toilsome road of life.
Her love of sin had brought regrets,
And heartaches sad, and strife.
She turned to Christ, and found real joy
And peace in serving Him.
But gone were all the wasted years,
N'er to return again.

I met a child along the way,
Bubbling with life and vim.
So eagerly she trusted Christ,
And gave her heart to Him!
Her faith was strong, her life was sweet;
She served Him all her days.
And many souls she led to Christ,
With lips brimful of praise.

It's wonderful to lead a *man*
To trust Christ as his Lord;
To see him turn from paths of sin,
And pray, and read God's Word,
But when a *child* in simple faith
Believes, and trusts God's Son,
How great the joy in Heav'n and earth.
A LIFETIME has been won!

A Smile As Big As All Outdoors

I was feeling out of sorts the day I met her,
I had troubles I would never understand.
Yet the reason that I knew I'd not forget her,
Was the way she looked at me and squeezed my hand,
    With a smile as big as all outdoors.

She was beautiful, and radiant, and glowing,
And I thought that she had never known a care.
At the time I had no earthly way of knowing
All the things she'd suffered, and would later share,
    With a smile as big as all outdoors.

I had scowled at life each time I had a problem,
Only smiling when all things had gone my way.
But she took time to listen and help solve them
As she showed me how to trust the Lord and pray,
    With a smile as big as all outdoors.

I have learned what matters most is how you take it,
When you face the irksome trials of daily life.
Now my smile is real—and I don't have to fake it,
As I rise above the things that cause me strife,
    With a smile as big as all outdoors.

I have found I need not fret about tomorrow;
I just trust the Lord to lead me day by day.
And no matter what may come, of pain or sorrow,
I will live my life to point men to the way,
    With a smile as big as all outdoors.

So I hope that even though I may not know you,
You will see the light of Jesus in my face,
As I look at you with love, and try to show you
How to find real peace by trusting in God's grace,
    With a smile as big as all outdoors.

Simplicity

I wish that I were silver tongued,
  And could express with eloquence
Magnificent soul-stirring thought.
I wish my words inspired such awe,
That all who heard would be amazed
At rhetoric my pen had wrought.

Instead I'm bound by simple rhyme,
Devoid of magniloquence,
To form my foolish words of praise.
And though they flow straight from my heart,
Sometimes they seem inept, obtuse,
As though they bear a strange malaise.

Still, Lord, I pray that You will use
My plain, unfancy doggerel,
To build in some lost soul a fire.
If You can bless my feeble thoughts,
And through them bring someone to You,
Then nothing else could I desire.

A Blanket Of Love

Adam, my two and a half year old grandson (pictured on cover) is constantly amazing us by the things he does and says. He has a special little soft blanket that is his favorite possession. He drags it around the house and holds on to it when he goes to sleep. He always wants it in close sight. He doesn't want to give it up, even when it needs washing.

His Mommy is expecting another baby in six months, and Adam is excited about the baby. One day his Mommy got some very sad news, and she started sobbing. Adam was so upset to see her cry that he got a Kleenex and crawled up into her lap, wiped away her tears and patted her cheek. "Don't cry Mommy," he said. "It will be all right." When she still cried he finally said, "Don't cry, Mommy. I'll give the baby my blanket."

We were all so touched that this sweet little child was willing to give up his most prized possession to help take away his Mommy's pain. It made me think about our precious Lord, and how He feels when He sees our tears. He tells us, "Don't cry. For I will give you My blanket of love. Your tears are very precious to Me, and I have saved each teardrop that has fallen from your eyes. Some day, because your sins have been covered by My blood, I will take you to your beautiful new home in Heaven where there will be no more tears and no more sorrow. Because I love you so much you can find security and peace in My blanket of love." How thankful I am that I have been given this security—His blanket of love.